WEST WYANDOTTE
KANSAS CITY KANSAS
PUBLIC LIBRARY

D1308421

DISCARD

Submarines

Use Place Value Understanding and Properties of Operations to Perform Multi-Digit Arithmetic

Noah Diedrick

PowerKiDS press.

NEW YORK

Published in 2015 by The Rosen Publishing Group, Inc.
29 East 21st Street, New York, NY 10010

Copyright © 2015 by The Rosen Publishing Group, Inc.

All rights reserved. No part of this book may be reproduced in any form without permission
in writing from the publisher, except by a reviewer.

Book Design: Mickey Harmon

Photo Credits: Cover Harry Hu/Shutterstock.com; pp. 3, 4, 6, 8, 10, 12, 14, 16, 18, 20, 22–24 (water) Andrea Danti/
Shutterstock.com; Photos courtesy of U.S. Navy: p. 5 Adam K. Thomas, p. 13 Peter D. Lawlor, p. 15 James Kimber,
p. 19 Ed Early; p. 7 (main) Anonymous/AP Images; p. 7 (inset) DEA PICTURE LIBRARY/Contributor/De Agostini/Getty Images;
p. 9 (main) Hulton Archive/Stringer/Hulton Archive/Getty Images; p. 9 (inset) http://en.wikipedia.org/wiki/File:British_WWI_
Submarine_HMS_R3.JPG; p. 11 Mariusz S. Jurgielewicz/Shutterstock.com; p. 17 Stocktrek Images/Stocktrek Images/Getty
Images; p. 21 (main) Dmitry Lovetsky/AP Images; p. 21 (inset) Hibrida/Shutterstock.com; p. 22 Ritu Manoj Jethani/
Shutterstock.com.

Library of Congress Cataloging-in-Publication Data

Diedrick, Noah, author.
Submarines : use place value understanding and properties of operations to perform multi-digit arithmetic / Noah
Diedrick.
    pages cm. — (Math masters. Number and operations in base ten)
Includes index.
ISBN 978-1-4777-4936-4 (pbk.)
ISBN 978-1-4777-4937-1 (6-pack)
ISBN 978-1-4777-6455-8 (library binding)
1. Place value (Mathematics)—Juvenile literature. 2. Addition—Juvenile literature. 3. Subtraction—Juvenile literature. 4.
Submarines (Ships)—Juvenile literature. I. Title.
QA141.3.D54 2015
513.2′1—dc23
                                        2014004363
Manufactured in the United States of America

CPSIA Compliance Information: Batch #WS15RC: For further information contact Rosen Publishing, New York, New York at 1-800-237-9932.

Contents

What Are Submarines?

A submarine is a kind of ship that can move on the surface of water as well as underwater. Submarines are the only kind of ship that can move underwater, so they look very different from other kinds of ships.

Submarines play important roles in navies around the world. The brave people who serve on submarines are called submariners. They have to live underwater for long periods of time in a submarine's close quarters.

Submarines have been used by navies for hundreds of years, but they didn't become a major part of warfare until World War I began in 1914.

Submarine History

During the **American Civil War** (1861–1865), a submarine was successfully used to sink another warship. On February 17, 1864, the *H.L. Hunley*, a Confederate (Southern) submarine, attacked and sank the Union (Northern) ship *Housatonic*. The submarine was also destroyed in the attack.

The *H.L. Hunley* used a **torpedo** filled with gunpowder in the attack. The torpedo was pulled behind the submarine at the end of a 200-foot line. If you added 2 of these lines together, what would the total length be?

You can use many different methods to add and subtract numbers. A common method is adding by place value. In this example, first add the 0 and 0 in the ones place. Then, add the 0 and 0 in the tens place. Then, add the 2 and 2 in the hundreds place. This gives you an answer of 400 feet.

Housatonic

$$200 \text{ feet}$$
$$+\; 200 \text{ feet}$$
$$400 \text{ feet}$$

H.L. Hunley

The most famous kind of submarine from World War I (1914–1918) was the German U-boat. A certain kind of U-boat, called a UA class boat, was 230 feet long. British R-class submarines were created to destroy U-boats. These submarines were only 163 feet long.

If 1 R-class submarine was placed directly behind 1 UA class boat, what would their total length be? What would the total length be if you put a UA class boat directly behind 1 R-class submarine?

As you can see, adding 163 to 230 gives you the same answer as adding 230 to 163. They both equal 393. This is an example of the commutative property of addition, which says that you can add numbers in any order and still get the same answer.

British R-class submarine

German U-boat

230 feet	163 feet
+ 163 feet	+ 230 feet
393 feet	393 feet

Submarine warfare was also a major part of World War II (1939–1945). The United States mainly used 2 kinds of submarines to fight battles in the Pacific Ocean: Gato-class and Balao-class. Balao-class submarines could dive deeper than Gato-class submarines. They could go up to 400 feet underwater.

If a Balao-class submarine dove 220 feet underwater and then went down another 175 feet, how far did it dive altogether? The answer is 395 feet.

You can break an addition problem into parts that are easier to work with. For example, 220 can be broken into 200 + 20, and 175 can be broken into 100 + 75. You can then add those numbers in whatever order is easiest.

$$220 + 175 = 200 + 20 + 100 + 75$$

step 1: 200 + 100 = 300

step 2: 20 + 75 = 95

step 3: 300 + 95 = **395 feet**

A New Kind of Submarine

After World War II, a new kind of submarine was created that could stay underwater for much longer periods of time. This kind of submarine was powered by a nuclear reactor, which is a machine that creates power from **atoms**.

Nuclear submarines commonly stay underwater for 90 days because that's how long the food supply lasts. If a nuclear submarine crew has been underwater for 75 days, how many more days do they have left underwater?

If you can't easily take 75 from 90, you can change the subtraction problem to an addition problem with a missing addend. Find the number that makes 90 when added to 75. The answer is 15.

90 – 75 = ? | ? + 75 = 90

90 – 75 = 15 | 15 + 75 = 90

U.S. Navy Submarines

Today, the U.S. Navy has 2 main classes of submarines. Attack submarines do just what their name says—attack enemy submarines. Fleet ballistic **missile** submarines, called "Boomers," carry large missiles but are created to stay away from other ships.

Attack submarines are 362 feet long, while Boomers are 560 feet long. What's the difference between these 2 lengths? You can subtract using place value to find the answer, which is 198 feet.

You can't take 2 from the 0 in the ones place, so you need to borrow from the tens place. The 6 in the tens place becomes 5, and the 0 in the ones place becomes 10. You can't take 6 from 5 in the tens place, so you need to borrow from the hundreds place. The 5 in the hundreds place becomes 4, and the 5 in the tens place becomes 15.

$$\begin{array}{r} \overset{4}{\cancel{5}}\overset{15}{\cancel{6}}\overset{1}{\cancel{0}} \text{ feet} \\ - \ 362 \text{ feet} \\ \hline 198 \text{ feet} \end{array}$$

Submarines used by the U.S. Navy can dive deeper than 800 feet underwater. If one submarine is 822 feet below the water's surface and another is 801 feet below the water's surface, what's the difference between how deep those submarines are?

You can use different methods to **solve** this equation, or math problem. You can subtract using place value. You can also find the number that makes 822 when added to 801. Using either method, the answer is a difference of 21 feet.

Many math problems can be solved in more than one way. You can choose the method that's easiest for you.

method 1:

822 feet
− 801 feet
─────────
  21 feet

method 2:

822 feet − 801 feet =   ? feet | ? feet + 801 feet = 822 feet

822 feet − 801 feet = 21 feet | 21 feet + 801 feet = 822 feet

Skilled Submariners

A U.S. Navy submarine crew isn't always the same size. However, most crews are made up of a group of 32 officers and **chief petty officers**, as well as 109 other sailors. How many submariners are on a U.S. Navy submarine altogether? You can use different methods to come to the same answer, which is 141.

Adding by place value with this equation is a way to practice carrying. When you add the 9 and 2 in the ones place, you get 11. That means you have to carry the 1 from the tens place in 11 to the tens place in the equation.

Women aren't allowed to serve on U.S. Navy submarines because there isn't enough privacy in such a small space.

$$\begin{array}{r} \overset{1}{109} \\ +\ 32 \\ \hline 141 \end{array}$$

method 2:

109 + 32 = 100 + 30 + 9 + 2

109 + 32 = 100 + 30 + 11

109 + 32 = 100 + 41

109 + 32 = 141

Submarines Around the World

There are 43 countries that have submarines as a part of their navy. The United States, United Kingdom, France, China, and Russia all have nuclear submarines. Other countries have much smaller and less advanced submarines.

There are over 600 submarines in use around the world today. If there are 381 submarines in 1 body of water and 212 in another, how many are in those 2 bodies of water altogether? What method would you use to solve this equation?

$$381 + 212 = ?$$

United Kingdom

Russia

China

France

Russia is the country with the largest number of submarines.

Important Jobs

Submarines have been a part of naval history for hundreds of years. It took a long time for people to build a submarine that could work properly and last. But now submarines have forever changed the way we fight wars and keep peace in the water.

Submarines help navies do many important jobs. They keep their countries safe from enemy submarines. They gather **information**. They help move people and supplies. And they even help find people stuck in or near the ocean!

People can take tours of some submarines that are no longer in use.

Glossary

American Civil War (uh-MEHR-uh-kuhn SIH-vuhl WOHR)
A war in the United States between the North and South
over slavery and other issues.

atom (AA-tuhm) A tiny bit of matter. Everything that exists is
made of atoms.

chief petty officer (CHEEF PEH-tee AW-fuh-suhr)
A high-ranking naval officer.

information (ihn-fuhr-MAY-shun) Knowledge or facts
about something.

missile (MIH-suhl) An object that is thrown, shot, or launched
to hit something far away.

solve (SAHLV) To find an answer.

torpedo (tohr-PEE-doh) A thin weapon shaped like a tube
that's launched by a submarine and can push itself
through water.

Index

Due to the changing nature of Internet links, The Rosen Publishing Group, Inc., has developed an online list of websites related to the subject of this book. This site is updated regularly. Please use this link to access the list: www.powerkidslinks.com/mm/nobt/sub